Third Edition

by Jonathan D. Kantrowitz

Edited by Ralph R. Kantrowitz

Item Code QWK2299 • Copyright © 2011 Queue, Inc.

Queue, Inc., 80 Hathaway Drive, Stratford, CT 06615
(800) 232-2224 • Fax: (800) 775-2729 • www.qworkbooks.com

Table of Contents

FILL IN THE MISSING WORD

Filling in the missing words is what this book is all about.

You will read a sentence that has had a word taken out. There will be a blank like this _____ where the word was. Your job will be to pick which word belongs in the blank.

You will need to pick which word makes the most sense in each sentence with a blank. You will be given five choices. Fill in the missing word by circling the letter of the correct answer. Here's an example with just two answer choices:

1. The _____ comes up every day.   a) song   b) sun

Read the sentence and the answer choices. Does a "song" come up every day? That doesn't sound right. Does the "sun" come up every day? That does make sense. The correct choice is **b**, sun. Circle the correct answer like this: (b) sun

Here is another one with four choices:

2. I read a _____ to my little brother last night.

    a) cook   b) look
    c) book   d) back

Read each of the answer choices. Try reading each one in the sentence. Which answer makes the most sense? It is **c**, book. That's what you would read to someone.

OK, now try these on your own:

3. In the winter, she loves to go _____ on the frozen pond near her house.

    a) swimming   b) skiing   e) dancing
    c) biking   d) skating

What do you do on ice? The answer to 3 is **d**, skating.

4. The fireman _____ a ladder to rescue the cat.

    a) chased   b) climbed   e) lit
    c) painted   d) walked

What do you do with a ladder? The answer to 4 is **b**, climbed.

Now here is one that is a little harder:

5. It was the middle of summer. The sun was high in the sky. Nothing was moving. It was very _____.

    a) raining   b) cloudy   e) windy
    c) hot   d) cold

"The sun was high in the sky" tells you that it wasn't **a**, raining or **b**, cloudy. "It was the middle of summer" tells you that it probably wasn't **d**, cold. Choice **e**, windy, is a possible answer, but "nothing was moving" doesn't fit with "windy." The best choice is **c**, hot.

Sometimes the right answer depends on what follows the blank. For example, look at the following question and answer choices:

6. My favorite room in my house is the _____. Everyone gathers there while my mom cooks dinner. It's warm and cozy and smells great.

a) attic   b) basement   e) playroom
c) kitchen   d) bedroom

Once you read past the blank you can tell that **c**, kitchen is the answer.

Here are some examples of how the sentence that follows the blank can change the answer:

7. The ball was _____. It was neither too large nor too small.

a) round   b) square   e) tiny
c) big   d) little

Only **a**, round would fit.

8. The ball was _____. It was so large, in fact, that I could hardly hold on to it.

a) round   b) square   e) thin
c) big   d) little

The answer would be **c**, big.

9. The ball was _____. It was so tiny I could hardly see it.

a) round   b) square   e) huge
c) big   d) little

The answer would be **d**, little.

Here is an example of the kind of passage and multiple-choice questions that you might find in a state reading test. The answers have been filled in for you.

Animals have babies just like people have babies. Animal babies, however, grow and act differently than human babies.

When lions have babies, they are called cubs. The lion cubs are _____**1**_____ by their mother for the first three months of their lives. After three months, the lion cubs eat the meat that other lions in their family collect. Lion cubs are very active and love to play. The cubs play with each other to get the _____**2**_____ they need to grow stronger.

A horse's babies are called fillies and colts. Fillies are the young female horses and colts are the young male horses. Fillies and colts grow very _____**3**_____. They need a lot of food to give them energy for so much fast growing. Some young horses can drink up to three gallons of milk a day! When horses are three or four years old, they are adults and can be trained by humans.

1 ○ watched   ○ moved
   ○ washed   ● fed
      ○ met

HINT: *To fill in this blank with the correct word, you have to look at the words in the next sentence. The next sentence says, "After three months, the lion cubs eat the meat that other lions in their family collect." The sentence is discussing how the lion cubs eat. The sentence with the blank says, "The lion cubs are _____ by their mother for the first three months of their lives." You need to choose the answer choice that has to do with eating. "Fed" is the best answer.*

2 ○ vitamins   ○ weight
   ○ time   ● exercise
      ○ nutrition

HINT: *To choose the right word in blank 2, you need to look at the words around this word. The sentence says that lion cubs play with each other to get something they need to get stronger. The previous sentence says that lion cubs are very active. Which of the answer choices is something that cubs would get from playing with each other and that they would need in order to grow stronger? "Exercise" fits best.*

3 ● quickly   ○ nicely
   ○ happily   ○ slowly
      ○ easily

HINT: *The words in the sentence with the blank will help you figure out the correct answer. This sentence says, "Fillies and colts grow very _____. The next sentence states "They need a lot of food to give them energy for so much fast growing." The word "fast" is a clue. You need to choose a word that means the same as fast. "Quickly" is a good answer. It makes sense in the sentence and means about the same as "fast."*

Now try it yourself with the passages on the following pages.

THE LEADING MEN OF QUINNIPIAC

Who were the leading men of the colony of Quinnipiac (New Haven)? Theophilus Eaton should be mentioned first. He was the wealthiest of all the founders. He was governor of the colony for as long as he lived. His house was probably the biggest in the town. It stood on the north side of Elm Street about halfway between Church and State Streets. He needed a ___1___ house because he had many people in his family. Besides his mother, wife, and children, there were several younger persons who had been placed under his care and protection. Including the servants, there were sometimes as many as 30 people in the house. It is said that 19 fireplaces kept this great house ___2___ in winter.

1 a) small   b) simple
    c) strange   d) large
         e) unknown

2 a) warm   b) safe
    c) loose   d) open
         e) dark

The main central room was furnished with fine carved tables, chairs, and carpets. In this room the whole family gathered for their meals and for prayers. Mr. Eaton also had a ___3___ and office where he loved to spend much time in reading and studying.

3 a) bathroom   b) library
    c) garden   d) garage
         e) pool

His brother Samuel ___4___ next door near the corner of State Street. Samuel did not remain in New Haven long. He returned to England, which is where he died.

4 a) fixed   b) lived
    c) ran   d) painted
         e) stood

The land belonging to Mr. John Davenport, the minister, was across the street from Mr. Eaton's. His house was also big and stately. It contained 13 fireplaces. One of the most interesting rooms in this house was the study. Mr. Davenport had a lot of ___5___ for those days. He spent much of his time reading them. The American Indians called him "so big study man." Nothing was done in the new colony without first asking his ___6___. All the people loved him and respected him.

5 a) tables   b) chairs
    c) money   d) pets
         e) books

6 a) name   b) father
    c) friend   d) dreams
         e) advice

Among the rest of these "first settlers" was George Lamberton. He was a famous sea captain. Nathanael Turner was the commander of the military company. Robert Newman owned the great barn where the settlers met to form a ___7___ to help provide rules and structure for the colony.

7 a) government   b) model
    c) clan   d) town
         e) mission

1

PEOPLE AND PLACES OF NEW HAVEN COLONY

Thomas Gregson was a leading man in the colony of New Haven. His lot was on the corner of Church and Chapel Streets. His house was one of the largest in the town. He was a merchant. In 1644, he was chosen to go to England and get a charter for the colony. The ship he sailed on was ____1____ at sea. It was never seen again.

1 a) lost   b) always
   c) floating   d) comfortable
          e) first

William Andrews kept the first "ordinary," or hotel. John Cooper looked after the fences every week. Francis Newman was a lieutenant in the military. He became governor after Mr. Eaton died.

For two years after the settlement of the town, Quinnipiac was the only name it had. In 1640, the General Court decided to give it a ____2____ name. The old record of that year says, "This town now called New Haven." By that time, it had grown to a population of nearly 500 people. It also had become the mother of other settlements.

2 a) foreign   b) new
   c) silly   d) healthier
          e) long

A group of people came from Herefordshire, England. They were ____3____ the southwest quarter of New Haven. They all moved to Wepowaug in 1639. There they built a town of their own. They named it Milford.

3 a) thrown   b) sent
   c) given   d) tossed
          e) taken

A year later, a number of families from Kent, England, moved to Menunkatuck. There they founded Guilford. At about the same ____4____, some people from Norfolkshire, England, went across to Long Island. There they built the town of Southhold.

4 a) time   b) block
   c) century   d) country
          e) moment

In 1640, New Haven ____5____ the territory at Rippowams from the American Indians. The land was between Hartford's colony, Fairfield, and the Dutch in Manhattan. The same year, they sold the land to a company that came from Wethersfield, Connecticut. This new settlement was named Stamford.

5 a) borrowed   b) bought
   c) left   d) loaned
          e) snuck

In 1644, Totoket was settled by a ____6____ company from Wethersfield. It was given the name Branford.

6 a) loud   b) same
   c) narrow   d) mean
          e) different

All these new towns ____7____ with the town of New Haven. They were all under the same government. They formed the "New Haven Colony."

7 a) united   b) fought
   c) divided   d) mixed
          e) argued

2

INSECTS THAT ARE NOT HARMFUL—Part I

It's a natural reaction to be frightened by some insects. Insects often look very scary. Many insects have the ability to hurt people. However, many large insects are not ___1___ at all.

1 a) awful   b) likable
    c) big   d) harmful
       e) friendly

Daddy-long-legs look like long-legged spiders. They are actually ___2___ of spiders, so they are alike in many ways. But, they do not sting or have venom, a type of poison. They only have one body section. Spiders have two body sections. Daddy-long-legs feed on plants and sometimes decaying materials found in forests.

2 a) enemies   b) followers
    c) fans   d) relatives
       e) made

Millipedes cannot hurt people. They do look similar to centipedes, but they are ___3___ in a few ways. First, millipedes have chewing mouthparts. Second, millipedes have two pairs of legs for each body segment. Centipedes have only one pair of legs per segment.

3 a) different   b) unique
    c) funny   d) twins
       e) strange

Millipedes are scavengers. They feed on either living or decaying plant parts near the forest floor. Many species are able to give off a foul-smelling fluid. It is toxic to insects, but won't do any damage to ___4___ because we are too big.

4 a) ants   b) bugs
    c) beetles   d) ladybugs
       e) humans

Dragonflies are some of the largest insects. They are ___5___ insects because they eat smaller insects such as mosquitoes and crop pests. Eating these other insects helps protect people and the flowers in their gardens. They hold their captured prey in their legs and munch on them while flying.

5 a) useful   b) ugly
    c) scary   d) strong
       e) mean

Despite old folktales that claim that they sew up your ears or your lips, dragonflies do not attack people. If you happen to catch one and hold onto it, it might pinch, but it won't break the ___6___.

6 a) bond   b) promise
    c) bank   d) bone
       e) skin

During its first stage of life, this insect lives underwater in streams and lakes. The dragonfly feeds on insects that live in the water and on other arthropods. Baby insects of some of the larger species even feed on small ___7___. Dragonflies in this stage can't hurt people either.

7 a) mammals   b) fish
    c) dogs   d) creeks
       e) trees

INSECTS THAT ARE NOT HARMFUL—Part II

Dobsonflies are very large. The adults especially have very large fanglike mouthparts. However, these mouthparts are not used to __1__. They are used only in trying to attract females. These insects are actually quite peaceful. The baby stage of this insect is known as a hellgrammite. It lives under rocks near water. It will give a good nip if you pick it up, but it is not __2__.

May beetles, June beetles, and Japanese beetles belong to a very closely related group of beetles called scarabs. People in Egypt thought scarabs were good luck. Beetles may __3__ into and land on people. They can't __4__ humans. But if you catch them and won't let them get away, they may give a slight pinch.

Cockroaches have been hated and feared for centuries. Historically, they have been linked with poor housing and dirty conditions. However, these insects can actually be found in any type of structure, even __5__ houses. They do not have any biting or stinging ability. So, although they may be ugly, they do not bite humans.

Cockroaches can be found in filthy and well-kept areas. They pose a threat to human __6__. They carry disease-causing bacteria. They leave it on surfaces or food. People may also develop severe allergies to cockroaches.

Praying mantids are predators of several crops and garden pests. They are also called praying mantis. Although they look quite threatening, they are not. They may make good __7__, in fact, as long as they are well-fed with smaller, soft-bodied insects and water is available. Otherwise, they are best left in a garden, working at keeping pests away.

1 a) eat   b) fight
   c) talk   d) whisper
       e) whistle

2 a) friendly   b) dangerous
   c) scared   d) happy
       e) peaceful

3 a) swim   b) squeeze
   c) fly   d) sink
       e) slither

4 a) hurt   b) upset
   c) like   d) heal
       e) annoy

5 a) clean   b) apartment
   c) big   d) haunted
       e) colorful

6 a) hearts   b) habits
   c) emotions   d) friends
       e) health

7 a) pets   b) companions
   c) siblings   d) mothers
       e) teachers

4

INSECTS THAT ARE NOT HARMFUL—Part III

Walking sticks are well ____1____. That's exactly what they look like! They are plant feeders. They have no ability to hurt humans. They make great pets. Be sure to provide them with plenty of plant material for them to eat.

Grasshoppers are grass feeders. They normally want nothing to do with humans. When handled, they may spit out a brown liquid as a scare tactic. They may also pinch with their mandibles (jaws). But their jaws are not ____2____ enough to do any damage. Other than that, grasshoppers do not pose a threat.

Silverfish are household pests that live in cracks that are warm and ____3____ like those near sinks and drains. They feed on starchy substances. They have no directly harmful effects on humans.

Many caterpillars found feeding on leaves are not harmful. They may be handled and even raised. However, any caterpillars with hairs or spines should be left alone or handled with extreme care. Wear gloves! Often, caterpillar spines are very ____4____. They can cut a person's hand and they sometimes contain a chemical irritant.

A few exceptions are woolly worms (woolly bear caterpillars) and the hickory horned devil. The devil is a caterpillar with very large projections. It is not harmful at all. In general, though, it's better to be safe than sorry.

Butterflies and moths are beautiful and ____5____ creatures. When caught, they will probably put up a fight by fluttering their wings. That can be unnerving, but it isn't harmful. If a butterfly lands on a person, it is possible that it just wants a sip of his or her ____6____, which contains salts that butterflies need. Their mouthparts are only modified to suck nectar and other liquids. They will not bite or sting.

Cicadas are large, distinctive creatures. They are common in late summer. They make very loud, unnerving ____7____, especially when disturbed. This can be heard from far away. They do not feed as adults and, other than being loud, will not bother people.

1 a) named   b) liked
   c) fed   d) raised
          e) known

2 a) strong   b) wide
   c) small   d) tall
          e) open

3 a) moist   b) creaky
   c) old   d) cool
          e) crooked

4 a) hairy   b) sharp
   c) cold   d) spicy
          e) hot

5 a) spiteful   b) hairy
   c) doubtful   d) graceful
          e) random

6 a) fingers   b) sweat
   c) milk   d) flowers
          e) soda

7 a) signs   b) scratches
   c) punches   d) whispers
          e) noises

SOCIAL PHOBIA

Do you feel afraid and ____1____ when you are around other people? Is it hard for you to be at school?

Does This Sound Like You?

I have an intense ____2____ that I will do or say something and embarrass myself in front of other people.

I am always very afraid of making a mistake and being watched and judged by other people.

The threat of embarrassment makes me ____3____ doing things I want to do or speaking to people.

I am stressed for days or weeks before I have to meet new people.

I blush, sweat a lot, tremble, or feel like I have to throw up before and during an event where I am with new people.

I stay away from social situations such as school ____4____.

If you have some of these problems, you may have social phobia.

Social phobia is a real illness. It can be treated with medicine and therapy like other illnesses. If you have social phobia, you are very concerned about embarrassing yourself in front of other people. Your fears may be so ____5____ that you cannot do everyday things. You may have a very hard time talking to people at school. Your fear may even keep you from going to school on some days. You may worry that you will blush and shake in front of other people. You may believe that people are watching you, just waiting for you to make a ____6____. Even talking on the phone or using a public restroom can make you afraid. Many people are a little nervous before they meet new people or give a talk. But if you have social phobia, you ____7____ for weeks before. You may do anything to stay away from the situation.

1. a) excited   b) friendly
   c) driven   d) happy
   e) uncomfortable

2. a) hope   b) hunger
   c) happiness   d) fear
   e) greed

3. a) avoid   b) love
   c) like   d) question
   e) content

4. a) events   b) bells
   c) libraries   d) books
   e) learning

5. a) serious   b) weak
   c) silly   d) long
   e) odd

6. a) speech   b) mistake
   c) scene   d) dollar
   e) play

7. a) watch   b) hide
   c) wait   d) stare
   e) worry

6

DEPRESSION

Depression is an illness that affects the body, ____1____, and thoughts. About twice as many women suffer from depression as men. People who are depressed may feel hopeless, worthless, or very sad. They may have no energy or interest in doing anything.

Some people say that depression is an "empty, ____2____ feeling that won't go away." This is called clinical depression. It is different from feeling "blue" or down for a few hours or a couple of days.

Many things cause depression. Depression can run in ____3____. For example, if your mother gets depressed, you may be more likely to get depressed. Changes in your brain chemistry can cause depression. Dealing with painful events in your life can cause you to become depressed. Sometimes depression is caused by medications people take. Some illnesses such as Parkinson's disease, stroke, and hormonal problems can cause depression.

Some of the most common ____4____ of depression include feeling empty, sad, and anxious. Another common symptom is feeling restless and irritable a lot of the time. Depressed people often feel worthless, helpless, hopeless, and guilty. They also have little interest or joy in their lives.

People who are depressed sometimes can't ____5____. They usually wake up early in the morning. They might cry more than usual. They also might have trouble concentrating, remembering, and making decisions. If you or someone you know has some of these signs for more than two weeks, see your doctor.

So how is depression ____6____? Most people with depression get better when they get treatment. The two most common treatments for depression are medication and psychotherapy. Psychotherapy means talking with a trained counselor. Support groups can help. Sometimes just ____7____ treatment is used. Sometimes both are used; a person takes medicine and sees a psychotherapist.

1 a) shoes   b) rain
   c) mood   d) rules
        e) weather

2 a) happy   b) miserable
   c) glad   d) content
        e) upbeat

3 a) schools   b) families
   c) bunches   d) rivers
        e) towns

4 a) designs   b) pictures
   c) signs   d) names
        e) mentions

5 a) weep   b) sneeze
   c) shop   d) jump
        e) sleep

6 a) recognized   b) rated
   c) known   d) helped
        e) scored

7 a) exciting   b) one
   c) expensive   d) enough
        e) colorful

TAKE CHARGE OF YOUR HEALTH

You are going through a lot of changes. Your body is transforming and ___1___. Have you noticed that every year, you can't seem to fit into your old shoes anymore? Or that your favorite ___2___ are now tighter or three inches too short? Your body is on its way to becoming its adult size.

Along with your physical changes, you are also becoming more ___3___. You are starting to make more choices about your life. You are relying ___4___ on your parents and more on yourself and your friends when making decisions. Some of the biggest choices that you face are those about your health.

Maintaining a healthy diet and being active now may help prevent diabetes, high blood pressure, heart disease, osteoporosis, stroke, and some forms of cancer when you are older.

Now is the time to take charge of your health by ___5___ better and being more physically active. Even small changes will help you look and feel your best!

Even if health issues run in your family, it doesn't mean that you will have the same problems. To learn more about your health, start by looking at your family. Are your parents, brothers, or sisters overweight? Do any of them have health problems related to their weight, such as type-2 diabetes? Your family's gene pool, dietary habits, and activities can all play a role in your health and the way you look.

Type-2 diabetes is increasing in adolescents and teenagers who are overweight. Diabetes means that blood glucose (blood sugar) is too high. Diabetes is ___6___. It can hurt your eyes, kidneys, heart and blood vessels, gums, and teeth.

Even if members of your family have type-2 diabetes or other health issues, it doesn't mean that you will have the same problems. To ___7___ your chances of developing them, keep your diet healthy and stay very active.

1 a) shrinking   b) growing
   c) hopping   d) sleeping
          e) spinning

2 a) shoes   b) games
   c) hats   d) jeans
          e) places

3 a) confused   b) immature
   c) fancy   d) independent
          e) famous

4 a) more   b) heavily
   c) wider   d) much
          e) less

5 a) eating   b) playing
   c) skipping   d) seeing
          e) singing

6 a) mean   b) peculiar
   c) serious   d) exciting
          e) strong

7 a) try   b) lower
   c) increase   d) raise
          e) steady

8

FINDING THE TILE DRAIN

One hundred seventeen acres of cropland used to be a farm. Then a public-spirited group decide to return it to its natural ____1____ of a wetland. It is now covered in native grasses. The field has rolling hills and a small creek. You can sometimes find birds called pheasants and deer in the undergrowth. However, challenges below the surface are making the wetland restorations ____2____.

In many wetlands, drainage tile was put in under the land. The tile helped to dry up the land. It created better drainage. Water could now flow beneath the ____3____ instead of being stuck on top of the ground.

Restored wetlands will not stay wet until the drainage tile is plugged or removed. Finding drainage tile is the problem. In most cases, no one has the original tile ____4____ or knows where they are. Photos taken from the air can provide an approximate location of existing tile.

The common practice for finding field tile is to probe the soil. Probers use a four- to five-foot steel rod. They go back and forth in a planned ____5____ until tile is found. Then the tile is exposed with a backhoe. It can take from hours to days to expose a dense array of drainage tile.

But what if you could see what was under the ground? Well, with a special ____6____ you can! It is called Ground Penetrating Radar (GPR). GPR was successful in finding buried tile 80% of the time in a study at Ohio State University.

A Minneapolis company called the National Ground Penetrating Radar Service recently volunteered to find buried drainage tile on the WRP site south of Good Thunder. Before this the company had used GPR to ____7____ underground tanks, burial plots, and steel reinforcement in hardened concrete. The company pulled its antenna across the ground. By doing this, they developed a computer image.

1 a) size   b) garden
   c) environment d) group
           e) crop

2 a) surprising   b) silly
   c) difficult   d) fun
           e) wonderful

3 a) surface   b) dirt
   c) bridges   d) sun
           e) moon

4 a) color   b) maps
   c) material   d) weight
           e) name

5 a) song   b) rhythm
   c) meeting   d) time
           e) pattern

6 a) tool   b) signal
   c) secret   d) clock
           e) code

7 a) build   b) hide
   c) locate   d) trap
           e) bury

THE ERIE CANAL

Jesse Hawley was a miller in the town of Geneva, New York. He was one of the first persons to propose a canal across the state of New York. President Thomas Jefferson thought the ____1____ was "little short of madness."

Dewitt Clinton was then mayor of New York City. He supported the canal. Clinton's opponents called the proposal "Clinton's Folly." In 1817, Clinton became governor of New York. Funds for a canal from the Hudson River to the Great Lakes were ____2____ approved. On July 4, 1817, workers broke ground in Rome, New York. Then they started west. This spot was chosen because no locks or aqueducts that would ____3____ progress were needed for approximately eighty miles. This helped quiet those against Clinton's idea.

The Erie Canal ("Clinton's Big Ditch") opened on October 26, 1825. It was hailed as the greatest engineering marvel in the world. It was 363 miles long and forty feet wide. It was only four feet deep. It included 18 aqueducts and 83 locks. The canal ____4____ travel time form the east coast to the Great Lakes by half. It reduced shipping costs by 90%.

The Great Lakes were the gateway to the west. The Erie Canal opened the only trade ____5____ west of the Appalachians. This caused the first great westward migration of American settlers. It turned Rochester, New York into the nation's first boom town.

The Hudson River was at the eastern end of the Erie Canal. New York City was down the Hudson River. The Erie Canal made New York City the busiest ____6____ in the United States.

The Erie Canal was enlarged three times, in 1862, 1895, and 1918. The canal today is 363 miles long. It has 57 locks. The total rise from the Hudson River to Lake Erie is 568 feet.

Shortly after the opening of the Erie Canal, branches to the canal were built to ____7____ other important water routes. These branches ensured that towns along previously used waterways were not abandoned. Today, the New York State Canal System extends over 524 miles and connects with hundreds of lakes and rivers.

1 a) speech   b) story
   c) idea   d) book
     e) tale

2 a) not   b) quickly
   c) since   d) never
     e) partly

3 a) speed   b) keep
   c) quicken   d) improve
     e) slow

4 a) shortened   b) increased
   c) lengthened d) worsened
     e) canceled

5 a) winds   b) materials
   c) route   d) booth
     e) driveway

6 a) court   b) house
   c) path   d) port
     e) part

7 a) connect   b) trick
   c) block   d) divert
     e) confuse

FISH NEED NURSERIES TOO!

Fish are many things to many people. Some types of fish are major sources of food. Commercial fishermen depend on fish for their livelihoods. So do businesses that promote fishing as a sport. Because fish are so ____1____, we should learn about them so that our activities will not harm them.

1 a) interesting   b) tasty
    c) numerous   d) smelly
        e) important

Several common types of fish depend on nursery areas within North Carolina sounds and rivers. These fish include flounder, spot, croaker, and menhaden. Nurseries are places for tiny juvenile fish and shellfish to mature and ____2____. They stay there until they are large enough to have families of their own.

2 a) shrink   b) grow
    c) ripen   d) celebrate
        e) fly

During the cold winter months, flounder, spot, croaker, and menhaden travel in the ocean toward the Gulf Stream. The Gulf Stream is a large current of clear, ____3____ water carrying heat up from the tropics. It is located approximately 25 to 50 miles off the North Carolina coast.

3 a) warm   b) green
    c) wide   d) salt
        e) dark

Near the Gulf Stream, the adult fish lay their eggs. They do so during the coldest time of year. The eggs are fertilized and drift in the ocean where they ____4____. The ocean is like a big delivery room. Currents take these tiny fish toward the coast. They travel through inlets in the outer banks such as Oregon Inlet, Hatteras Inlet, and Ocracoke Inlet.

4 a) die   b) swim
    c) scramble   d) hatch
        e) jump

After entering the sounds, or areas of water, the tiny fish travel with the currents to coastal streams, rivers, bays, and grass beds. These places are called nursery areas because tiny fish and shrimp stay there while they are very ____5____. Food and shelter are ____6____ in these areas. They live in the nursery areas during the late winter, spring, and early summer and grow very quickly. These nursery areas are filled with the food baby fish need to grow.

5 a) hot   b) large
    c) hungry   d) slow
        e) young

6 a) scarce   b) rare
    c) expensive   d) plentiful
        e) cramped

From midsummer to fall, the partially grown fish and fully grown shrimp ____7____ the nursery areas and enter the open sounds and the ocean.

7 a) paint   b) drink
    c) destroy   d) betray
        e) leave

ANNIE OAKLEY

Annie Oakley was born on August 13, 1860, in Darke County, Ohio, the fifth daughter of Jacob and Susan Moses. After her Quaker family's tavern in Hollidaysburg, Pennsylvania had burned, they moved to Ohio. Jacob Moses died from an illness in 1866. For the next several years, Annie helped her family by ____1____ chores on the family farm. She also trapped and hunted small animals for food.

At the age of eight or nine, she went to ____2____ at the county poor farm. A poor farm was a place where individuals who could not support themselves could go. They would work on the farm to earn their keep. At one point during her stay, she was "lent out" to a local farm family as a servant. According to her autobiography, the family that took her in abused her mentally and physically. After two years, she ran back to the poor farm. She ____3____ there until she was thirteen or fourteen. While at the poor farm, she learned to sew and received a general education.

When Annie returned to her family, she found that they had been suffering through a very ____4____ period. Annie's mother had remarried. This second husband had died after leaving her with a new child. Annie's mother was then married a third time. Even with this remarriage, the family ____5____ were not very good. The family was about to lose their farm because they could not afford it.

Upon Annie's return home, she used her father's Kentucky rifle to hunt small animals. She sold what she ____6____ in Greenville and to hotels and restaurants in northern Ohio. Before leaving for the poor farm, she had taught herself how to do these things.

Annie was so ____7____ at hunting that she was able to pay for the family farm with the money she had earned from the sale of her animals. In the book she wrote about herself, she notes, "Oh, how my heart leaped with joy as I handed the money to mother and told her that I had saved enough to pay it off!" At the time, she was fifteen.

1 a) skipping   b) avoiding
   c) forgetting   d) performing
        e) escaping

2 a) shop   b) dance
   c) live   d) sing
        e) eat

3 a) remained   b) grew
   c) slept   d) sat
        e) left

4 a) happy   b) joyful
   c) confusing   d) familiar
        e) difficult

5 a) stories   b) chances
   c) pets   d) garages
        e) finances

6 a) fired   b) shot
   c) won   d) bought
        e) cleaned

7 a) bad   b) useless
   c) average   d) unnatural
        e) successful

12

QUANAH PARKER SURRENDERS

Chief Quanah's final _____1_____ came at a trading post called Adobe Walls. It was on the South Canadian River. It was about sixty miles west of the Oklahoma boundary line. The great chief would suffer a serious injury in the battle.

The date was June 25, 1874. A party of buffalo hunters had taken refuge there. A band of 700 Comanches and Kiowas, under the ___2___ of Quanah, charged them several times. The tribes were held back, but lost many men. Quanah himself was badly ___3___. They finally gave up in defeat

Over time, one by one, the tribes surrendered. Quanah and his men held out. A post at Fort Sill had been built several years before. It was watched over by troops of the United States Army. They were told to watch the movements of the tribes. Finally, Quanah began to march to this fort to surrender when he had no other choice. The flag of truce was waved. The Comanches under Quanah were the _____4_____ American Indians of the southern plains to make peace with the whites. Everyone else had done so already.

Shortly after his surrender, Quanah went to Texas to visit relatives and the grave of his mother. It was at this time that he added "Parker" as his last name.

However, even after making a treaty, Quanah Parker didn't ___5___ the white man's ways. He kept his tribe from adopting white ways and the Christian religion.

The Plains tribes were forced to live on reservations. Quanah and a part of his tribe once left their reservation without _____6_____. They went out to the Texas Panhandle country to spend the winter in Palo Duro canyon. When spring came, a group of soldiers were sent out to find Quanah and bring him _____7_____. The soldiers arrived at the edge of the canyon just as Quanah's group came up from below to return to the reservation.

A fight started before Quanah knew the soldiers were there. He immediately galloped out between his own people and the soldiers. He explained that they were not at war. He said that they would quietly return to the reservation.

1. a) traffic   b) message
   c) trade   d) battle
       e) meeting

2. a) arm   b) leadership
   c) umbrella   d) thumb
       e) promise

3. a) outnumbered   b) insulted
   c) tempered   d) armored
       e) wounded

4. a) first   b) oldest
   c) only   d) last
       e) strangest

5. a) dismiss   b) forget
   c) like   d) remember
       e) exchange

6. a) permission   b) practicing
   c) thinking   d) help
       e) shoes

7. a) coffee   b) back
   c) horses   d) blankets
       e) food

QUANAH PARKER AND HIS WIVES

Quanah Parker was given a piece of land. It was four miles northwest from Cache, Oklahoma. A home had been built for him there. It had 22 rooms.

Rooms for each one of Quanah's wives were furnished identically so that none of his wives could ____1____ that one had a better room than the other. During his lifetime, Quanah recognized seven different wives, but he never had more than five at one time. Whenever Quanah Parker went to town or made ____2____ on special occasions, he used a large stagecoach drawn by four mules. He often took all of his wives along and some of the children. At fairs and celebrations, this stagecoach, with all the pomp and pride of its owner, was frequently seen.

In 1892, the Commissioner of Indian Affairs approached Quanah in regard to the ____3____ of wives he would be allowed to keep. Their conversation was mainly as follows: "Quanah, you have agreed to take allotments and sell your surplus lands and let them be ____4____ by white people. When the white people come to be your neighbors it will be the white man's law and the white man's law says one wife. You have too many wives. You will have to ____5____ which one you want to keep and tell the rest of them to go somewhere else to live."

Quanah listened attentively and looked at the commissioner with a very fixed gaze for some moments. Then he retorted, "You tell um!" He waited several ____6____ until the significance of this had dawned on the commissioner's mind. Then he added, "You tell me which wife I love most—you tell me which wife love me most—you tell me which wife cry most when I send her 'way—then I pick um."

The commissioner replied, "Oh, let's talk about something else." In time, Quanah fought with one wife and then another, and "threw them away." That was the American Indian ____7____ for divorce. At the time of his death, he had just two left.

1 a) observe   b) complain
   c) decide   d) write
          e) realize

2 a) quilts   b) meals
   c) trips   d) cakes
          e) sandwiches

3 a) names   b) kind
   c) mothers   d) age
          e) number

4 a) run   b) managed
   c) ridden   d) settled
          e) photographed

5 a) decide   b) vote
   c) guess   d) write
          e) cover

6 a) years   b) moons
   c) decades   d) lifetimes
          e) moments

7 a) picture   b) song
   c) color   d) dance
          e) phrase

14

MULTICOLORED ASIAN LADY BEETLE

Arrival Date: This lady beetle came from Asia. It was introduced to the U.S. in 1916 to control insect pests. Populations were slow to grow in the United States until 1988. Then a ____**1**____ population was noticed in New Orleans. Since then, the ___**2**___ of Asian lady beetles has continued to grow.

Multicolored Asian lady beetles can be ___**3**___ insects. They do a great job of controlling aphids. This is called "biocontrol". Aphids can damage many types of plants. The beetles reduce the need for damaging pesticides, chemicals that kill insects. Despite this benefit, the beetles swarming outside homes or ___**4**___ around inside bother people!

How to Identify: The multicolored Asian lady beetles ___**5**___ like common "ladybugs." They have many shades of color. They generally have more spots than native lady beetle species. Sometimes they don't have spots at all. Look for the big false "eyes." These are two white football-shaped spots behind the head. Also look for their mustard-yellow or red coloration.

Metamorphosis: Lady beetles go through four stages of life over an average of 20 days. They start as eggs. Then a beetle changes to a larva, pupa, and an adult with wings. Eggs are laid on host plants. There the larvae can feed on aphids and other arthropods. Beetles are known to ___**6**___ about 300 aphids before they become adults!

Multicolored Asian lady beetles like many plants. These include evergreens, apple and maple trees, alfalfa, wheat, cotton, tobacco, and small grains. Larvae molt four times before becoming pupae. These beetles can make up to five generations in areas with extended periods of warm weather. Adult beetles can live for as long as two to three years.

Evidence of Invasion: In the fall, adult beetles will search for ___**7**___. They want a safe place to spend the winter. They cluster in big groups in autumn on sunny southwest sides of light-colored rock outcroppings, at the base of logs, tree trunks, or the walls of buildings—like your house!

1 a) large   b) smelly
    c) loud   d) diverse
      e) tall

2 a) size   b) number
    c) reputation   d) body
      e) appetite

3 a) harmful   b) dangerous
    c) helpful   d) expensive
      e) annoying

4 a) driving   b) sailing
    c) swimming   d) marching
      e) flying

5 a) sound   b) travel
    c) look   d) move
      e) mature

6 a) eat   b) hurt
    c) hate   d) lick
      e) fight

7 a) food   b) water
    c) fun   d) grass
      e) shelter

OH, DEER!

It is ___1___ in many states to feed deer. People could get in a lot of trouble for doing it. In the winter, deer herds tend to move to lower land closer to homes and businesses. Some people may feel the deer do not have enough food sources in the wintertime. They believe that adding to their diets grain, corn, or hay is helpful. In fact, the opposite is ___2___.

Feeding deer can be dangerous for them. "People who feed deer do more harm than good," says Trina Lynch. She is a wildlife manager.

There are several reasons why it is forbidden to feed deer. One important reason is that deer are the main food of mountain lions. "Concentrating deer by feeding can ___3___ mountain lions well within the city limits. It may become necessary to kill these lions for public safety," Lynch says.

The normal feeding behavior of big game animals allows them to ___4___ out as they graze or browse. Artificial feeding disrupts that behavior. It prompts deer to crowd together in small areas. In these areas, they are more likely to be ___5___ by dogs and hit by cars.

Deer have a complex digestive system. They can not easily digest bread and many types of hay. "Becoming used to artificial feeds that do not meet their nutritional needs often results in deer that are in ___6___ condition," explains Bob Davies. He is a wildlife biologist.

Causing deer to group together by putting food out can also increase stress on the deer. It can speed the spread of disease.

Although commercial foods for wild animals are available at many stores, biologists warn against them. "Some of these ___7___ may indicate they will attract certain wildlife species, including deer," said Davies. "People should be aware that if they place food out, and deer consume it, they may be breaking the law. Fortunately, once people learn about the negative impacts that occur when deer are fed, most stop doing it," he said. "The few people that continue to feed cause problems for the deer and for their neighbors."

1. a) wise   b) useful
   c) helpful   d) illegal
   e) fun

2. a) wrong   b) telling
   c) true   d) extreme
   e) funny

3. a) show   b) sell
   c) attract   d) repel
   e) eliminate

4. a) work   b) spread
   c) go   d) jump
   e) fall

5. a) chased   b) eaten
   c) broken   d) licked
   e) warned

6. a) top   b) strange
   c) strong   d) hard
   e) weak

7. a) products   b) signs
   c) restaurants   d) boxes
   e) nutrients

WATER FLOWING IN THE EVERGLADES

The Everglades is surprising. Look out across the vast ___1___ of grass as you drive through the park. It is hard to imagine that what you are looking at is a river.

The "River of Grass," as the Everglades is sometimes called, flows only six inches deep in most places. However, it may swim sixty miles wide across the flat landscape. The water drifts ___2___ along under the hot sun. Slowly but surely, it flows southward toward the ocean.

During the winter dry season, this flood of water slows down to a ___3___. A few deeper channels carry the life-giving water through the marsh. They keep alive the many different plants and animals that depend on the water to live.

Taylor Slough is the name of one such channel. It flows along the eastern edge of Everglades National Park, until it reaches Florida Bay, at the tip of the Florida peninsula. The flow of the Taylor Slough dilutes this warm, shallow bay to a salt level only half that of the open ocean.

Fish, shrimp, and lobsters ___4___ in Florida Bay under these conditions. In turn, they keep alive a major commercial fishing industry in the Florida Keys. Rare and endangered manatees and sea turtles also stay safe in Florida Bay.

But for many decades, Taylor Slough has not carried the amount of water it did historically. Humans have ___5___ the flow of water through the River of Grass for almost a hundred years. Dikes were built around parts of Lake Okeechobee as early as 1931.

By the middle of the century, long ridges and canals crossed the south Florida peninsula. The water of the Everglades was captured so that people could use it. It was used for drinking, flood control, and to water crops. Too little ___6___ water flowed into Florida Bay. Its plants and animals began to die. Bit by bit, over the last half century, Taylor Slough has dried up from the hot Florida ___7___.

1 a) sea   b) dirt
   c) pictures   d) museum
       e) signs

2 a) rapidly   b) quickly
   c) massively   d) passionately
       e) lazily

3 a) trickle   b) point
   c) stop   d) dam
       e) halt

4 a) thrive   b) die
   c) suffer   d) smell
       e) sink

5 a) ignored   b) increased
   c) swallowed   d) changed
       e) sampled

6 a) cold   b) fresh
   c) soda   d) dirty
       e) ice

7 a) sun   b) birds
   c) stove   d) soil
       e) land

BLACKBEARD BEGINS

Little is known of Blackbeard's early life. That was the case with most pirates. Pirates did not want their ___1___ to be embarrassed. It is believed that Blackbeard was born around the 1680s in Bristol, England. He is said to have been born to respectable, well-to-do parents. He was a very ___2___ man. He could read and write with much skill. He was at ease with governors as well as others of high classes.

He served England as a privateer in Queen Anne's war. That was a war between France and England. Privateers were private ships and crewmen who aided the English navy. They stopped and looted merchant ships of other countries. They claimed that this was to prevent supplies from reaching the ___3___.

The war ended in 1714. After the war, many people who had made good livings as privateers for their country were out of ___4___. Some of them turned to being pirates. This was the case with Blackbeard.

In the late summer of 1716, Blackbeard took a job with Captain Benjamin Hornigold as a pirate. Blackbeard quickly became skilled at ___5___ in the Caribbean waters. Then in 1717, after a successful raid, Captain Hornigold presented Blackbeard with his own ship.

Blackbeard renamed the ship *Queen Anne's Revenge*. Next came the task of outfitting the ship as a pirate ship. Men had to be found and trained. Then Blackbeard set about making a reputation for himself.

Blackbeard wanted to be ___6___ by one and all. He traveled the waters off the Caribbean and Atlantic coasts. He soon was ___7___ cargo and threatening passengers, crewmen, and even other pirates. He left almost nothing behind him.

1 a) competitors   b) teammates
   c) neighbors   d) teachers
        e) families

2 a) angry   b) lazy
   c) nasty   d) educated
        e) violent

3 a) stores   b) top
   c) enemy   d) bottom
        e) mall

4 a) school   b) work
   c) time   d) food
        e) bullets

5 a) swimming   b) standing
   c) sailing   d) moving
        e) rafting

6 a) liked   b) loved
   c) feared   d) teased
        e) surprised

7 a) camping   b) selling
   c) lifting   d) burying
        e) stealing

18

DOOMED PROJECT

Rene-Robert de la Salle was a famous French explorer. He decided to build forts along the mouth of the Mississippi River. From there, he hoped to __1__ and conquer Spanish areas in Mexico.

1 a) assist   b) invade
    c) build   d) befriend
      e) help

To accomplish his goal, he thought he would need an army of 200 Frenchmen, 15,000 American Indians, and privateers. La Salle's enemies doubted his plan. But King Louis XIV saw it as a good chance to strike out against Spain, with whom France was at war. The king gave his fellow Frenchman men, ships, and money.

The mission was a series of __2__. La Salle and the naval commander of the Navy did not get along. La Salle had a strong personality and demanded the most of himself and of others. Often he pushed people to their limits and became upset when they would argue with him. He was not a good __3__. He was almost never on friendly terms with his men, so they rarely wanted to follow him.

2 a) triumphs   b) victories
    c) miracles   d) failures
      e) episodes

3 a) sailor   b) teacher
    c) captain   d) friend
      e) child

After a stop in the West Indies, one ship was captured by pirates. Many sailors also got sick and died. At the time, __4__ were difficult to follow. Therefore, La Salle missed the mouth of the Mississippi River. He landed at Matagorda Bay in Texas, nearly 500 miles away.

4 a) maps   b) trains
    c) streets   d) books
      e) cars

While trying to make his way through the narrow passageways of the inlets, a second ship, the *Amiable*, sank. Valuable cargos of food, medicine, supplies, and trade goods for the American Indians were __5__. A third __6__, the *Belle*, became stranded on a sandbar in a storm. Several men drowned as they tried to get away from the ship.

5 a) lost   b) secured
    c) gained   d) trusted
      e) found

6 a) box   b) canoe
    c) raft   d) plane
      e) boat

La Salle made several attempts to __7__ his error. But he was never able to lead his group to the Mississippi. He established Fort St. Louis in present-day Victoria County, Texas. But there was not much more success than that. La Salle was a man of great vision, but he lacked leadership ability. The building of a French empire in the New World would be left to other men.

7 a) wrong   b) correct
    c) dismiss   d) forget
      e) ignore

THE CAYUSE TRIBE

The social organization of the Cayuse tribe was a loose one. The basic unit was the family. Each was ___1___ by a father whose decisions were final. His authority was independent of the chiefs or elders.

Several families formed a band. Several of these bands made the tribe. There was no head chief for the whole tribe. Each band had its own chief. He held his ___2___ by inheritance, merit, or wealth, or by a combination of these. A chief was an ___3___ person, but he was not a dictator over the actions of his band. For hunts or warfare, a chief would often grant his ___4___ to the most experienced hunter or warrior. In addition, each band had a group of elders who offered advice. To some extent, they managed the common affairs of the band under the direction of the chief.

The Cayuse were good at selective horse breeding. Large, well-bred horse herds enriched the tribe. The herds gave the tribe power that far exceeded its small size. The horses also made the American Indians very ___5___. In the appropriate seasons, they were able to cross the mountains to the east to hunt and rode down the Columbia River to fish at Celilo Falls.

Hunts were composed of organized groups. They hunted deer, American elk, pronghorn, bison, and smaller animals. Meat that was not ___6___ fresh was made into a highly concentrated, nutritious type of food called pemmican.

During the time when there were many salmon, nets, weirs, spears, hooks, and baskets were all used to catch the big fish. The Cayuse women ___7___ some of the fresh salmon on sticks over a fire. The rest they sun-dried, pulverized, and packed into baskets for winter use.

In addition, the Cayuse collected berries and roots in the mountains. Berries were preserved by being pressed into dry cakes or by being mixed with pemmican. Camas bulbs were dug in large quantities, steamed in pits, and formed into cakes that were dried in the sun. These cakes were eaten as bread or boiled into mush.

1 a) destroyed   b) seen
   c) headed   d) spent
       e) hidden

2 a) ground   b) gun
   c) head   d) position
       e) side

3 a) influential b) angry
   c) old   d) ignorant
       e) adorable

4 a) shirt   b) food
   c) books   d) weapons
       e) leadership

5 a) big   b) wealthy
   c) weak   d) mobile
       e) happy

6 a) caught   b) shipped
   c) bought   d) ordered
       e) eaten

7 a) buried   b) roasted
   c) chopped   d) burned
       e) boiled

20

MOSES AND HER PEOPLE

Harriet Tubman helped 300 people to freedom. She helped ____1____ members of her own family. Among them were her 70-year-old parents. At one point, rewards for Tubman's capture totaled $40,000. Yet, she was never captured. She never failed to deliver her travellers to safety. As Tubman herself said, "On my Underground Railroad I [never] run my train off track. I never [lost] a ____2____."

1 a) buy   b) employ
    c) sell   d) hire
       e) rescue

2 a) battle   b) passenger
    c) dime   d) thing
       e) patient

During the Civil War, Tubman worked for the Union army as a nurse, a cook, and a spy. Her contributions were very valuable. Her experience leading slaves along the Underground Railroad was especially ____3____. She had been everywhere. She knew the land well. She brought in a group of former slaves to hunt for ____4____ camps. They also were to report on the movement of these Confederate troops. In 1863, she went with Colonel James Montgomery and about 150 black soldiers on a gunboat raid in South Carolina. Because she had inside information from her scouts, the Union gunboats were able to ____5____ the Confederate rebels.

3 a) useless   b) harmful
    c) helpful   d) dangerous
       e) interesting

4 a) summer   b) enemy
    c) soccer   d) rabbit
       e) tennis

5 a) impress   b) select
    c) film   d) surprise
       e) arm

At first, when the Union Army came through and burned plantations, slaves hid in the woods. But then they realized that the gunboats could take them behind Union lines to freedom. They came running from all directions, each bringing as many of their ____6____ as they could carry. Tubman later said, "I never saw such a sight."

6 a) belongings   b) bags
    c) friends   d) pots
       e) tools

Tubman worked as a nurse during the war, trying to heal the sick. Folk remedies she learned during her years living in Maryland came in very handy. At the time, many people in the hospital died from a disease called dysentery. Doctors did not have a cure.

Tubman was sure she could help cure the sickness if she could find some of the same flowers and herbs that grew in Maryland. One night, she searched the woods until she found water lilies and geranium. She boiled parts of the water lily and the herbs. It made a bitter-tasting brew. She gave it to a man who was dying. It worked! Slowly he ____7____.

7 a) swallowed   b) slipped
    c) worsened   d) faded
       e) recovered

     21

BAD BREATH

Bad breath, or halitosis, can be caused by many things. It may be the result of ____1____ odor-causing foods like onions or garlic. But for many of us, the cause is tooth decay, gum disease, dry mouth, inadequate oral hygiene, or a medical disorder.

If you don't brush and floss daily, particles of food remain in the mouth, gathering bacteria that can cause bad breath. Food that ____2____ between the teeth, on the tongue, and around the gums can rot, leaving an unpleasant odor. Remember to clean your tongue, too!

Saliva is the mouth's natural mouthwash. To keep your saliva flowing, drink plenty of water. Water provides the fluid needed to keep your mouth ____3____. Rinse your mouth before ____4____ to dampen oral tissues before you sleep.

You might also try chewing foods like carrots and celery. Chewing generates saliva. Chew, for example, sugar-free gum. Chew for ____5____ periods. Long chewing periods may encourage other dental problems.

Avoid sleeping flat. It blocks saliva from flowing to your stomach while you sleep. This can lead to bad breath caused by reverse stomach acid flow. Use a pillow to raise your head so ____6____ and your saliva can work together.

Many people damage their teeth by brushing too hard! It doesn't take much pressure to remove bacteria, food, and plaque from your teeth. But many people apply three to four times the pressure necessary for effective ____7____. They are at risk of receding gums, sensitive teeth, notched teeth, and root cavities.

It takes 2–3 minutes to correctly brush your teeth well. Brushing your teeth for a longer time is far more effective than brushing harder. Most people spend only 30 seconds brushing.

Brushing longer—not harder—is the key to removing bacteria. Check with your dentist for more tips on good ways to brush your teeth.

1 a) buying   b) roasting
   c) eating   d) drying
     e) being

2 a) collects   b) grows
   c) jumps   d) peeks
     e) develops

3 a) warm   b) open
   c) wide   d) cool
     e) moist

4 a) school   b) sports
   c) activity   d) bedtime
     e) spitting

5 a) active   b) short
   c) endless   d) large
     e) lasting

6 a) thinking   b) calories
   c) gravity   d) waking
     e) pushing

7 a) whistling   b) cleaning
   c) talking   d) depositing
     e) moving

DANGEROUS INSECTS AND THEIR RELATIVES—Part I

Insects that have the ability to bite or sting will usually not do so if left alone. They will bite or sting only when mishandled or otherwise ___1___.

1 a) mistreated   b) missing
  c) ignored   d) mocked
     e) fed

Centipedes are not actually insects, but they are closely related to insects. They have long flattened bodies. They have at least fifteen pairs of legs. They also have fangs, which can inflict a ___2___ attack.

2 a) massaging b) scratchy
  c) painful   d) loving
     e) tickling

Centipedes can be distinguished from the similar but harmless millipedes. They have fangs instead of chewing mouthparts. They have one pair of legs per body segment. Millipedes have two pairs of legs per body segment.

Ticks are also insect relatives. They can be found in wooded areas or fields with tall grass. Ticks are very small and many are hard to ___3___. Once female ticks bite, they swell up with the blood of the host. The best way to keep from getting bitten is to tuck pant legs into socks and to wear loose-fitting clothing in areas that may have ticks.

3 a) like   b) miss
  c) see   d) understand
     e) believe

Ticks are dangerous because of the ___4___ they may carry. These include Lyme disease and Rocky Mountain spotted fever. Ticks often do not attach ___5___. Instead, they walk around over the skin until they come to a tight place, such as around the waist or wherever clothing is tight on the body. Check yourself or have someone else check you for ticks as often as you can. That way, you can ___6___ any before they bite.

4 a) grudges   b) food
  c) illnesses d) lice
     e) venom

5 a) strongly   b) smoothly
  c) wisely   d) properly
     e) immediately

6 a) bunch   b) bother
  c) charge   d) scout
     e) remove

If a tick does attach to the body, do not try to pull it off with your fingers. The mouthparts may break off underneath the skin. It is better to use a clean pair of ___7___. Grasp the tick as close to the front of the head as possible. You should try to pull the tick off with its mouthparts intact.

7 a) scissors   b) teeth
  c) pants   d) tweezers
     e) toes

23

DANGEROUS INSECTS AND THEIR RELATIVES—Part II

Lice are highly modified insects. They have no wings. Their legs are modified to move through animal or human hair. The best way to protect yourself from lice is to maintain healthy hygiene and not sharing things that go through your hair, such as ___1___, combs, hats, etc.

Fleas are pests of dogs, cats, and livestock. They have legs that can ___2___ over relatively long distances. That helps them hop from one animal to another. They also have comb-like body parts. These help the insects resist being brushed out of hair. The young or larvae are very tiny worm-like creatures. They can be present on fabric, carpet, or outdoors.

Both adults and larvae are present outdoors, where pets have been, in warm weather. Fleas generally do not prefer humans. However, they may try to feed on humans if they have been ___3___ for a long period of time. Fleas have also been known to carry diseases, such as black plague. Those fleas usually infest rats. There is not a lot of risk of those types of ___4___ in the United States at this time.

Bees will not generally attack people. However, when people get too close to the hive or swat at the worker bees, workers may ___5___ in defense.

If bees are flying nearby, the best strategy is to stand still or run away. Swatting may only make bees mad. Sometimes people have allergic reactions to bee stings. These may include rapid tissue swelling and difficulty breathing. If this happens, seek medical attention immediately. This could be a life-threatening situation if the person is highly allergic to bee venom.

Bees and wasps that live alone also have to find things for their offspring to eat. If you leave them alone, they will probably leave you alone. Some wasps may be more aggressive in the fall when less ___6___ is available. Be aware that honey bees can only sting once, but wasps are able to sting ___7___.

1 a) gloves   b) conditioner
    c) shoes   d) water
       e) brushes

2 a) jump   b) kneel
    c) skip   d) stretch
       e) slide

3 a) starved   b) smashed
    c) beaten   d) bored
       e) caught

4 a) birds   b) illnesses
    c) pets   d) bugs
       e) mice

5 a) hiss   b) lick
    c) sting   d) swerve
       e) flee

6 a) shelter   b) wood
    c) food   d) autumn
       e) sun

7 a) hard   b) sharply
    c) easily   d) slowly
       e) repeatedly

DANGEROUS INSECTS AND THEIR RELATIVES—Part III

Stag beetles are related to scarabs. However, they are a little more aggressive than scarabs. The males have very large mouthparts called mandibles. They can inflict a very painful pinch if they are ___1___.

Blister beetles can also be ___2___, especially to livestock like cows and sheep. Their blood contains a substance called cantharadin. It will cause blisters if it comes in contact with ___3___ or is swallowed.

Mosquitoes are very well-known pests. Only the females bite. They need blood to reproduce. What actually ___4___ when mosquitoes bite is the saliva that is injected while the mosquito inserts her mouthparts under the skin. This can be annoying, but scratching the bite may cause it to become infected.

Hellgrammites are another name for baby dobsonflies. These larvae live in streams. Unlike the adults, the larvae's large mouthparts are quite functional and can inflict a painful bite. Use forceps or a twig to move them rather than ___5___ them, if possible. If you must handle them, be careful!

Earwigs can be found in warm, damp basements and garages. They have two tail-like appendages that look very much like tweezers. If bothered or threatened, they may try to inflict a pinch, which can be painful. They may also spray a foul-smelling liquid as a means of ___6___.

All spiders have venom that is used to paralyze their prey so they can't move. The black widow spider is black with a red hourglass on the underside of its abdomen. The toxins in its venom will make people who are bitten very ___7___. Prompt medical treatment is recommended.

The brown recluse is a light brown spider with a darker brown fiddle shape on its back. A bite from this spider is dangerous. The toxins in its venom cause tissue surrounding the injury to die and rot. For some people who are highly sensitive to the toxins, a brown recluse attack can be a life-threatening situation. Seek medical attention right away.

1 a) happy   b) cold
    c) mishandled   d) soft
       e) weak

2 a) useful   b) helpful
    c) harmful   d) interesting
       e) friendly

3 a) hair   b) clothes
    c) tables   d) skin
       e) fingernails

4 a) itches   b) pricks
    c) tickles   d) scabs
       e) soothes

5 a) touching   b) torching
    c) pulling   d) tasting
       e) pushing

6 a) play   b) defense
    c) fun   d) attraction
       e) communication

7 a) big   b) angry
    c) smart   d) young
       e) sick

A MAMMOTH DISCOVERY

Two men crawl and climb along a rocky ledge near the ceiling of the cave. They move carefully so they will not fall to the cave floor ___1___. Both are experts at moving around in the cave. They have been tour guides for many years.

One of the men decides to go around a large boulder. He slips for a moment. He catches his balance by putting his hand down to steady himself. He has done this dozens of times before. This time, however, something ___2___ different. Rather than the usual rough and jagged surface of the ledges, he touches something smooth and rounded. He calls his companion to come and look. To the ___3___ of the two guides, the dim light of their kerosene lanterns reveals the faint outline of the top of a man's head. It is sticking out from beneath the large boulder. Quickly the men ___4___ the cave. They want to find others to come and see their discovery.

That year, 1935, proved to be one of the most exciting years for archeological research in Mammoth Cave's history. The two guides, Lyman Cutliff and Grover Campbell, had found what archaeologists would determine was the well-preserved body of a man. He had visited the cave almost 2,000 years before. Their studies showed that the man had indeed been on the ledge looking for something when he was ___5___ beneath the large boulder. With the help of the Civilian Conservation Corps, archaeologists lifted the heavy boulder with ___6___ and pulleys. That revealed the entire body.

The physical evidence showed that the man belonged to a group of people archaeologists refer to as "Early Woodland." They were people who hunted game and gathered wild foods in the eastern woodland forests. They were also the first farmers in the Green River Valley. They experimented with ___7___ gourds and sunflowers. The things that were found from these people, including cane reed torches, digging sticks, and sandals made from vegetable fibers "twined" together, have been found in many parts of Mammoth Cave.

1 a) above   b) around
   c) across   d) ceiling
        e) below

2 a) feels   b) sounds
   c) shouts   d) fills
        e) smells

3 a) annoyance   b) anger
   c) amazement   d) confusion
        e) fear

4 a) clean   b) fill
   c) march   d) leave
        e) sweep

5 a) robbed   b) resting
   c) living   d) trapped
        e) called

6 a) windows   b) cars
   c) ropes   d) string
        e) bikes

7 a) hunting   b) eating
   c) gathering   d) growing
        e) burning

26

AWARD WINNERS OF 2006

Union, Westport, and West Hartford, Connecticut have won awards for highest voter turnout. The award is ____1____ every year to the small-, mid-, and large-sized towns with the best voter turnout on Election Day.

1 a) given   b) left
c) taken   d) spotted
     e) thrown

These three towns did the best job in 2006 of getting voters out to the polls. All three showed very ____2____ voter turnout for a mid-year election.

2 a) high   b) spirited
c) poor   d) smart
     e) weak

We had a very interesting mix of winners this year. Union is the state's smallest town. It is a winner for the first time. Westport won the award for mid-sized towns for the second time. West Hartford continues its great Election Day work every year. This was its fifth ____3____ among large-sized towns in seven years.

3 a) loss   b) helping
c) try   d) choice
     e) victory

There is no civil right we have that is more important than our right to vote. These three towns did a wonderful job this year of leading the ____4____ for Connecticut. I congratulate the citizens of Union, Westport, and West Hartford for their great work this year.

4 a) battle   b) reading
c) way   d) light
     e) weight

Towns with less than 15,000 voters are small. Towns with 15,000 to 30,000 voters are mid-sized. Cities and towns with more than 30,000 voters are considered large.

Connecticut's voters have ____5____ that democracy is still strong. Connecticut's voters were interested and involved right from the beginning of this year. The turnout was ____6____. Voters were certainly motivated to follow the issues this year. Campaign rallies had more of an old-fashioned feel to them this year. That was especially true in the United States Senate race. There were plenty of stump speeches and voter-to-candidate contact.

5 a) doubted   b) wondered
c) proven   d) explained
     e) suspected

6 a) slow   b) sad
c) outside   d) excellent
     e) unusual

Thomas Fitzgerald is First Selectman of Union. He said, "Winning the award is wonderful. We're a very close-knit town up here. Everybody knows everybody. We all get together on Election Day and always produce a good turnout. There is a lot of community ____7____ up here. People want to have a voice and they want to have a say."

7 a) people   b) pride
c) tension   d) houses
     e) color

CONNECTICUT IS UNITED

The colony of Manhattan had been beaten and taken from the Dutch. Its name was ____1____ to New York. Many of the New Haven people who had thus far opposed the union with Connecticut now favored it. They believed that if the two colonies were ____2____ there would be more chance of their keeping the new charter and their rights. The town of Milford soon voted to join Connecticut. This weakened New Haven still more. Guilford and Branford were the only towns left. Many of the people in those towns were beginning to ____3____ the union.

Then the Royal Commissioners decided to give Long Island to New York. They fixed the boundary between New York and Connecticut where it is today. This act placed New Haven in the Connecticut colony. That made it necessary for the colony to give up its ____4____. A meeting of the General Court was therefore held. The New Haven Colony voted to submit to Connecticut.

Most of the people soon forgot the bitter quarrel and were content with their new government. But some were still unhappy. The people of Branford were so ____5____ that they soon left their town. Under the leadership of Mr. Pierson, their minister, they moved to New Jersey and founded the city of Newark. Robert Treat of Milford was another founder of Newark.

But there was no one in old New Haven who was as disappointed over the union with Connecticut as Mr. Davenport. His great ambition and cherished hopes were destroyed forever. He was _____6_____ and would not be comforted. In the year 1668, he moved to Boston where he became the minister of the old First Church. Two years later, he passed away.

But the city he left in sorrow, and which owes so much to him, has neither ____7____ nor stopped respecting his name. And the blessings, which resulted from the union he tried so hard to prevent, have long since replaced the wrong that helped to bring it about.

1
a) surrendered
b) given
c) moved
d) sold
e) changed

2
a) lost
b) divided
c) united
d) moved
e) conquered

3
a) dislike
b) hate
c) fight
d) support
e) sell

4
a) leaders
b) money
c) flag
d) citizens
e) independence

5
a) angry
b) hungry
c) excited
d) pleased
e) surprised

6
a) devastated
b) scared
c) lonely
d) energized
e) joking

7
a) remembered
b) taught
c) forgotten
d) cared
e) honored

28

ARE YOU BEING BULLIED?

So you're being bullied, huh? That can feel pretty awful. But no matter how bad it makes you feel sometimes, you should know you're not ____1____. That's right . . . there are plenty of kids all over the world who go through the same things you do every day. And, even though you may feel ____2____ sometimes, there are lots of things you and others can do to stop the bullying. Give these tips a try.

Always tell an adult. It's hard to talk about serious things with adults sometimes, but they can help put a stop to bullying. Tell an adult that you ____3____ and can talk to. It could be your parents, your teacher, your school counselor, your coach, or your neighbor. If you've told a grown-up before and he or she hasn't done anything about it, tell someone else. If you're afraid to tell an adult that you have been bullied, get another person—like a friend, sister, or brother—to go with you.

Having someone else there to ____4____ you can make it a lot less scary. Tell the adult exactly what has happened—who did the bullying, where and when it happened, how long it's been happening to you, and how it is making you feel.

If you talk with an adult at your school, ask him or her what they will do to help stop the bullying. It is his or her ____5____ to help keep you safe. Most adults really care about bullying and will do everything they can to help you.

Stay in a ____6____. Kids who bully like to pick on kids who are by themselves a lot. It's easier and they're more ____7____ to get away with their bad behavior. When you spend more time with other kids, you are not such an easy target. You'll also have others around to help you if you get into a difficult situation!

1 a) sick   b) mean
    c) weak   d) alone
        e) alert

2 a) helpless   b) dizzy
    c) strict   d) happy
        e) silly

3 a) dislike   b) trust
    c) met   d) see
        e) need

4 a) support   b) watch
    c) pinch   d) play
        e) move

5 a) dream   b) job
    c) time   d) turn
        e) joke

6 a) library   b) hotel
    c) house   d) box
        e) group

7 a) excited   b) likely
    c) eager   d) afraid
        e) welcome

29

NEW HAVEN AND THE AMERICAN INDIANS—Part I

The ____1____ of New Haven began their settlement at Quinnipiac in 1638. Mr. Theophilus Eaton and Mr. John Davenport, as they were wise and honest men, thought that Quinnipiac belonged to the American Indians who lived there. They did not think it would be ____2____ to stay there without paying the American Indians for the land. Thus, they wanted to obtain a good title to the soil and the goodwill and friendship of their neighbors.

1 a) founders   b) streets
   c) colors   d) homes
       e) names

2 a) fun   b) cheap
   c) right   d) allowed
       e) hard

There were only a few American Indians living in the country around Quinnipiac in 1638. Great heaps of oyster shells found along the shore by the English proved that there had been a large number of them years before. But wars with other tribes, famine, and terrible diseases had killed them.

There were hardly enough people left to make one small ____3____. They were called the Quinnipiacs. Momaugin, the leader of the group, could only find 47 men and boys for his band of warriors. There were only a few women and children. They lived in what is now East Haven.

3 a) riot   b) route
   c) tribe   d) building
       e) trip

Beyond East Rock, there were a few more under the lead of Montowese. There were only 10 men among them. By 1639, there were probably as many—if not more—British people at Quinnipiac than American Indians.

These American Indians in the Quinnipiac area had been living in great fear of their _____4_____, the Pequots and especially the Mohawks. The Mohawks came from the Hudson River region. They treated the American Indians in Quinnipiac with great ____5____. They sometimes forced them to pay long strings of beads called wampum for taxes. So terrible was the war-whoop of a Mohawk to their ears that the Quinnipiacs had several times fled to the settlement at Hartford for ____6____.

4 a) animals   b) weapons
   c) waters   d) enemies
       e) buffalo

5 a) kindness   b) respect
   c) sadness   d) hope
       e) cruelty

6 a) fun   b) protection
   c) food   d) vacation
       e) canoes

Therefore, when the English came to live near these Quinnipiacs, and on their own lands, they were not ____7____. Instead, they welcomed the British as friends and protectors.

7 a) impressed   b) excited
   c) angry   d) sad
       e) amused

30

NEW HAVEN AND THE AMERICAN INDIANS—Part II

The Quinnipiacs had made it plain that the English would be welcomed. A price was offered for the American Indians' __1__. This was quite good for farming and starting a new community. They believed it to be a good deal. So, when Mr. Eaton arrived, they were ready to sign an agreement of sale, called a treaty.

It was some time before the actual purchase could be made, however. In the first place, the British had to find a man who could __2__ the American Indians' language. He would need to explain the treaty to the Quinnipiacs.

Also, they thought that it would be better to wait awhile and see how the American Indians __3__. Then they could judge better what the terms of the treaty ought to be. This was a very wise thing to do. Before the first summer had passed, the American Indians were found to be very __4__ neighbors. In fact, they were annoying.

The Quinnipiacs were not used to the __5__ of the English. They did some things that were very different from what the British were used to. They would walk right into the English homes without knocking or asking permission. They often stole fish from the English nets and used boats and canoes without permission. They set traps where the cattle would be caught and injured. They sometimes came into the town on Sunday to trade and would hang around the houses while the people were at church. They did not understand that these behaviors were not common for the white men. They did not share the same ideas about privacy and property.

Of course, the English did not want to allow such things to go on for very long. So, when the treaty was drawn up, Mr. Eaton made the American Indians agree not to act that way anymore.

Thomas Stanton of Hartford was the only white man living anywhere near Quinnipiac who could communicate in the American Indian language well. He came to New Haven to __6__ the treaty to the American Indians. It wasn't until the last day of November 1638 before Mr. Stanton arrived. Word was then sent to Momaugin. He and the leaders of his tribe came into the town to __7__ what the strange looking paper with the writing on it meant.

1 a) cattle　　　b) labor
　 c) boats　　　d) fish
　　　　e) land

2 a) speak　　　b) honor
　 c) write　　　 d) imitate
　　　　e) describe

3 a) spoke　　　b) behaved
　 c) worked　　 d) cooked
　　　　e) traded

4 a) respectful　b) thoughtful
　 c) secretive　 d) sweet
　　　　e) difficult

5 a) buildings　 b) clothing
　 c) habits　　 d) history
　　　　e) stories

6 a) send　　　 b) explain
　 c) sign　　　 d) complete
　　　　e) plan

7 a) feel　　　　b) trash
　 c) count　　　d) ignore
　　　　e) learn

　　　31

NEW HAVEN AND THE AMERICAN INDIANS—Part III

Mr. Stanton spoke in a loud, clear voice. He explained each word and sentence of the writing to the Quinnipiacs in their own language. When he finished, Momaugin __1__ the document. He did so by making his mark in the form of a bow. Several of his advisors also made their marks. Underneath these was the mark of Shampishuh, Momaugin's sister.

In the treaty, Momaugin said that he owned all the land in Quinnipiac and that he alone had the right to __2__ it. Then the treaty stated that the American Indians freely gave up to Mr. Eaton and the other Englishmen all right to all the land, rivers, ponds, and trees in Quinnipiac, as far as it extended east, west, north, and south.

In return for all this, the American Indians asked for only __3__ things. First, they wanted a place in what is now East Haven where they could live and plant their corn. Second, they asked for the right to hunt and fish in Quinnipiac. And third, they wanted __4__ from the Mohawks and their other enemies.

The American Indians had to __5__ not to set traps where cattle might be caught or hurt. They had to pay for __6__ they killed or injured and return those that strayed away. They were also asked not to frighten away or steal fish from the English nets.

They were not to come into the town on Sunday to trade or hang around the houses while the English were at church. They were not to open any Englishman's __7__ without permission. They also could not stay in the house when told to leave. They were not to take any boat or canoe belonging to an Englishman without the permission of the owner. Not more than six American Indians at a time were to come into the town with bows and arrows or other weapons. They also were not to harm any British man, woman, or child.

1 a) signed   b) crumpled
    c) hated   d) trashed
      e) tasted

2 a) install   b) sell
    c) plow   d) display
      e) paint

3 a) five   b) two
    c) ten   d) three
      e) seven

4 a) gifts   b) promises
    c) calls   d) favors
      e) protection

5 a) pretend   b) agree
    c) seen   d) claim
      e) refuse

6 a) crops   b) children
    c) cows   d) canoes
      e) crabs

7 a) floor   b) door
    c) pouch   d) hand
      e) chest

32

NEW HAVEN AND THE AMERICAN INDIANS—Part IV

The land purchased by the settlers was wild. It had to be ___1___ and made ready for use by the British.

The American Indians could not use all of the land for planting. It was really not worth much to them. They needed just a small place to ___2___ enough corn to support themselves. There were only about 100 American Indians living in the region. They could still hunt and fish. That was all they had ever done there.

The English settlers at Quinnipiac followed the agreements with the American Indians. They always treated their neighbors with justice and kindness. They wanted to keep them ___3___. They also felt that it was right to act that way.

If an American Indian was wronged or injured by a white man, justice was done. For instance, when a guide named Wash was ___4___ and had his arm broken by an angry sailor, the court sent the sailor to prison and ordered the doctor to care for the broken arm.

At another time, a man ___5___ some meat from an American Indian named Durance. The thief had to pay the man double the price of the meat. He also had to pay a fine to the town and sit in the jail awhile.

Once, the American Indians complained that the English people's hogs ate their corn and made their children cry. They asked the English to help them fence in their land to keep the hogs out. At the same time, a man named Sagamore asked the town to give him a coat because he was old, poor, and couldn't ___6___. So the town gave the poor warrior a coat. They also sent men who were "fit and able" to help build fences around the American Indians' cornfields.

As a result of these kind acts, no American Indian weapon was ever ___7___ against New Haven. War whoops were never heard in its streets.

1 a) planted   b) groomed
    c) flooded   d) cleared
       e) massaged

2 a) eat   b) grow
    c) sort   d) swallow
       e) roast

3 a) upset   b) quiet
    c) friendly   d) confused
       e) guessing

4 a) lost   b) looking
    c) pleased   d) standing
       e) attacked

5 a) gave   b) borrowed
    c) stole   d) sold
       e) cooked

6 a) sleep   b) jump
    c) work   d) speak
       e) dream

7 a) made   b) destroyed
    c) placed   d) purchased
       e) raised

COUGAR BIOLOGY AND BEHAVIOR

Cougars have been ___1___ a lot in the western U.S. and Florida. Here is some of what has been learned.

Size & Color: Adult males average around 140 pounds and seven feet from nose to tip of tail. The tail is almost as long as the body. Females are usually around 100 pounds and six feet. They are brown to gray above and whitish below. The young are born with spots that ___2___ during their first year.

Diet: Deer are their main food, but smaller animals such as raccoons, opossum, skunks, rabbits, beaver, coyotes, and rodents are also important, especially for ___3___ cats not yet experienced in hunting. Adult cougars kill an average of about one deer every seven to ten days. All parts are ___4___ except for bones, hair, and intestines.

Population Growth: Biologists call cougars "self-regulating." This means that they keep their own numbers low because they need large places to live. Deadly fighting between males and high death rates of young cougars also keeps the population low. Even in places where prey is easy to find, the number of cougars does not always ___5___.

Home Range: The home range of a cougar depends on the amount of food, ___6___ of other cougars, and type of land. A male's home range usually overlaps the range of several females, but usually not the range of another male. Female home ranges may also overlap.

Habits: Cougars are usually alone, except for mothers with young. Mating begins at about two years of age. It may take place at any time during the year. Young cougars stay with their mothers for up to two years. Female cougars often settle near their mothers, but male cougars roam widely in search of new home ranges. It is during this time of ___7___ that cougars are most likely to encounter humans.

1. a) taught   b) learned
   c) studied   d) eaten
   e) heard

2. a) mate   b) fade
   c) stain   d) jump
   e) sparkle

3. a) older   b) smarter
   c) bigger   d) slower
   e) younger

4. a) broken   b) touched
   c) seen   d) consumed
   e) licked

5. a) decrease   b) increase
   c) dim   d) compute
   e) count

6. a) mansion   b) house
   c) location   d) feelings
   e) father

7. a) birth   b) ambush
   c) travel   d) attack
   e) settlement

MEMPHIS ZOO SELECTED AS HOME FOR COUGAR KITTENS

Three tiny little cougar kittens were found all ____1____. They had lost their mother almost two weeks ago. But they stayed together. A Duvall homeowner found them near her home in late August. The kittens' mother was killed by a Washington Department of Fish and Wildlife (WDFW) enforcement officer on August 9. He had to shoot the adult cougar. She had attacked and killed small livestock. The kittens were found on August 21. They were believed to be about five weeks old.

1 a) twirling   b) sitting
   c) alone   d) crazy
     e) dancing

The kittens were delivered to the Progressive Animal Welfare Society (PAWS) Lynnwood facility the next day. It has now been ____2____ that the kittens will be transferred to the Memphis Zoo. They will all be able to live together there.

2 a) rumored   b) gossiped
   c) announced   d) lied
     e) joked

The Memphis Zoo was ____3____ after a nationwide search for a good place to put the kittens. The ____4____ is expected in two to three weeks. The cats will remain at the PAWS facility for a little while. They need to wait until state and federal health certificates and transfer permits are given.

3 a) lost   b) mistaken
   c) failed   d) chosen
     e) eliminated

4 a) money   b) move
   c) party   d) letter
     e) concert

Cougar experts say the kittens are too young to have all the ____5____ skills to be returned to the wild. The experts also looked into trying to raise the kittens and train them for later release into the wild. That was not found to be a good option. The experts did not think the cougars could learn the skills they needed without their mother to ____6____ them. WDFW then began a search for the best permanent home for the kittens.

5 a) survival   b) foraging
   c) mature   d) fighting
     e) communication

6 a) feed   b) teach
   c) pamper   d) nurse
     e) groom

"We appreciate the exceptional care that the cougar kittens have received at the PAWS Wildlife Center," said WDFW Director Jeff Koenings. "The dedication that PAWS staff have shown in treating these ____7____ cats has been nothing short of tremendous."

7 a) old   b) fake
   c) young   d) pesky
     e) broken

PAWS will transfer the kittens to WDFW once they have been given a clean bill of health. Animal handlers from the Memphis Zoo will fly to Seattle. They will then take the cougars to their new home.

    35

THE LAKOTA—Part I

The Dakota Nation includes the native peoples who once lived in the northern forests along the upper Mississippi River in northern Minnesota. In time, the Dakota Nation divided into ____1____ groups. They were the Dakota, Nakota, and Lakota. Each moved in different directions. They still kept close ties to one another.

1 a) two   b) five
    c) three   d) six
        e) four

The Lakota are one tribe of the Dakota Nation. The Lakota were the first of the Dakota to leave the forest. Their name means "forest dweller." They headed out west. There they lived a ____2____ life. They followed the buffalo. They depended on buffalo hunting for food, clothing, and shelter. They ranged far from their Minnesota homeland. Each summer, they brought back buffalo furs to ____3____ with tribes from southern Minnesota.

2 a) easy   b) disturbing
    c) traveling   d) angry
        e) constant

3 a) trade   b) dance
    c) tease   d) cook
        e) play

The Lakota are also known as the Western Dakota or Teton. When the Dakota Nation split, the Lakota moved from northern Minnesota to the plains north of the Black Hills to the Platte River. They also moved westward into present-day Colorado, Wyoming, and Montana. The Lakota are the largest division of the Dakota Nation. They are known as the great buffalo hunters of the west.

The Lakota lived in tepees in small family groups. The tepees were ____4____ because they could be easily transported to follow the buffalo. tepees were pointed structures. They consisted of poles covered by animal skin or cloth. Sometimes as many as 16–18 buffalo skins were ____5____ together for use as a teepee covering. The opening to the teepee was held together by wooden "pins." A smoke hole in the top of the teepee allowed ____6____ to be built inside.

4 a) useless   b) heavy
    c) pretty   d) convenient
        e) smooth

5 a) sewn   b) traced
    c) cut   d) burned
        e) drawn

6 a) beds   b) bows
    c) grass   d) fires
        e) shelters

Buffalo skins were used to make robes, teepee covers, clothing, moccasins, bags, carrying cases, and boxes. The working of skins was generally done by women. They would tan them, remove the hair, and transform them into ____7____ items.

7 a) heavy   b) hard
    c) foreign   d) live
        e) useful

Lakota clothing was made mainly of buffalo skins. The women would spend many hours decorating the clothing with beads, bones, or other natural objects of beauty.

THE LAKOTA—Part II

The Lakota were always on the move. They planted very few crops. They looked for ___1___ plants such as onions, potatoes, turnips, strawberries, gooseberries, grapes, plums, and sweet red prickly pears.

Along with what they could find growing naturally, the Lakota primarily hunted buffalo. They used the American Bison (buffalo) for their meat and hides. They used bows and arrows for hunting. They could shoot an arrow entirely ___2___ a buffalo.

Buffalo meat was often boiled in holes in the ground. It was then enjoyed during a hunting celebration following the return of the hunters. However, most buffalo meat was prepared for later use. Some was ___3___ in the sun to make jerky.

The Lakota's favorite way to eat buffalo was to make it into pemmican. To make pemmican, buffalo steaks were made. Then they were laid on a large, flat stone and pounded with smaller stones. When the meat had turned into powder, it was ___4___ with melted fat or marrow. The mixture was put into hide bags with melted fat poured on top to seal it. Buffalo prepared in this way could stay good for 3–4 years.

Like other Dakota groups, many Lakota bands would meet in the summer. They would hold political meetings, religious ceremonies like the Sun Dance, sporting events, marriages, and coming-of-age ceremonies. These ___5___ events were a great opportunity to see family members who were also member of other bands.

The Lakota got fast horses in the mid-1700s. They were excellent ___6___. The large number of horses they owned combined with their remarkable horsemanship resulted in their ability to travel longer distances than any of the other Dakota groups.

The Lakota would use a *travois*, the French word for shafts of a cart, for long-distance travel. The *travois* was made of two long ___7___. They were crossed and fastened above the shoulders of a horse with the ends dragging behind.

1 a) expensive   b) green
   c) wild   d) secret
     e) trading

2 a) around   b) through
   c) over   d) under
     e) into

3 a) held   b) dried
   c) waved   d) drained
     e) found

4 a) thawed   b) tied
   c) centered   d) surrounded
     e) combined

5 a) scary   b) annoying
   c) sad   d) special
     e) quiet

6 a) riders   b) trappers
   c) trackers   d) raiders
     e) traders

7 a) sides   b) fingers
   c) arms   d) poles
     e) tires

SNACK SMART FOR HEALTHY TEETH

Think about when and how often you eat snacks. Do you nibble on sugary snacks many times throughout the day, or do you usually just have dessert after dinner? ____1____ acids form in your mouth every time you eat a sugary snack. The acids continue to affect your teeth for at least 20 minutes before they are broken down and can't do any more harm. So, the more times you eat sugary snacks during the day, the more often you feed bacteria the fuel they need to cause tooth decay.

1 a) Damaging   b) Helpful
   c) Colorful   d) Slimy
      e) Tasty

If you eat sweets, it's best to eat them after a main meal instead of several times a day between meals. Whenever you eat sweets—in any meal or snack—brush your teeth well with a fluoride toothpaste afterward.

If you snack after school, before bedtime, or at other times during the day, choose something without a lot of sugar or fat. There are lots of good snacks that are less ____2____ to your teeth—and the rest of your body—than foods loaded with sugars and ____3____ in nutritional value.

2 a) attractive   b) tasteful
   c) kind   d) invisible
      e) harmful
3 a) extreme   b) topped
   c) packed   d) full
      e) low

Low-fat choices like raw vegetables, fresh fruits, or whole-grain crackers or bread are ____4____ choices. Eating the right foods can help ____5____ you from tooth decay and other diseases. Next time you reach for a snack, make up your own menu of non-sugary, low-fat snack foods from the basic food groups.

4 a) silly   b) naughty
   c) boring   d) unwise
      e) smart
5 a) remove   b) protect
   c) lift   d) transfer
      e) signal

Candy bars aren't the only foods that cause problems. Foods such as pizza, pretzels, and hamburger buns may also contain sugars. Check the label. The new food labels ____6____ sugars and fats on the Nutrition Facts panel on the package. Keep in mind that brown sugar, honey, molasses, and syrups also react with bacteria to produce acid, just as refined table sugar does. These foods also are potentially dangerous to teeth.

6 a) identify   b) speak
   c) color   d) inject
      e) illustrate

Next time ____7____ before you pop another piece of candy into your mouth, "Is this really the best snack for me to eat?"

7 a) laugh   b) think
   c) sing   d) yell
      e) pretend

38

NEW HAVEN SETTLERS REACH BOSTON

The good ship *Hector* and her companion carried those who were going to found New Haven. It set sail from London, England sometime in April 1637.

The ____**1**____ across the Atlantic in those days was very long and tiresome. The ships were small and ____**2**____. It was often cold and rainy. The wind whistled through the rigging so shrilly that it frightened the children. Of course, many were seasick. The food was bad. They could have no fresh meat or vegetables. There was no room for the children to run about and the sailors liked to play jokes on them.

The journey usually lasted two months. Sometimes it was much longer. Everybody was _____**3**_____ when land was reached. They would get out and stretch their legs. They would also finally have something fresh to ___**4**___ and drink.

Mr. John Davenport and Mr. Theophilus Eaton with their company of Puritan colonists reached Boston in June 1637. When they had left England, Mr. Davenport did not know in what part of New England they would settle. They decided to ___**5**___ in Boston awhile. They would remain there until they could decide just which place they wanted to settle.

Their Boston friends urged them to remain in that city. They were even offered a place for a new town wherever they might choose. But they did not care to stay in Massachusetts for several ____**6**____.

First, there was an argument in the church at Boston over a woman named Ann Hutchinson, who was preaching some new and strange ideas. Everybody was excited about her. Mr. Davenport did a great deal to quiet this excitement and put an end to the argument. He and Mr. Eaton both ____**7**____ that their people would become mixed up in similar religious arguments if they remained in Massachusetts.

Secondly, they wanted to found a colony of their own where they could govern themselves in their own chosen way.

1 a) movie   b) music
   c) voyage   d) line
      e) memory

2 a) beautiful   b) inviting
   c) warm   d) large
      e) uncomfortable

3 a) relieved   b) disappointed
   c) confused   d) concerned
      e) shocked

4 a) sing   b) eat
   c) gargle   d) settle
      e) smell

5 a) set   b) sit
   c) stay   d) cartwheel
      e) stand

6 a) months   b) mistakes
   c) dollars   d) reasons
      e) years

7 a) wanted   b) worried
   c) liked   d) craved
      e) hoped

THE FOUNDERS OF NEW HAVEN ARRIVE

About 250 persons came to New England with Mr. Davenport and Mr. Eaton. Of these, about 50 were men. The rest were ____1____, children, and servants. By the time they were ready to leave Boston and go to Quinnipiac, many Massachusetts people had joined them. So, the small boat that carried them from Boston to their new home was pretty ____2____.

As the founders of the future ____3____ of New Haven entered the harbor of Quinnipiac that April day in 1638, how strange everything looked to them and how different from today!

No lighthouses guided the sailors. No breakwater sheltered the bay. No ____4____ of steel crossed over the rivers. Only wilderness bordered the way.

Coming slowly up the harbor, they ____5____ around eagerly and curiously. Toward the east, they saw hills covered with small oak trees. Toward the west were great forests of pines. In later years, one of New Haven's popular shore resorts would be named after these forests. In the distance were the Red Hills, as the Dutch called them, now known as East Rock and West Rock.

After they passed the mouth of the West River and neared the head of the harbor, the sailors saw two deep creeks extending far into the country and at almost right angles to each other. They called one of these East Creek and the other West Creek. Both have entirely ____6____. The tracks of a great railroad lie in the dry bed of one and the other has become a busy street.

Small ____7____ could enter the East Creek as far as the corner of the present State and Chapel Streets. But the Puritan settlers sailed up the West Creek. Their friends, who had spent the long winter there, were waiting for them. They made a camp near what is now the corner of George and College Streets.

1 a) horses   b) dogs
   c) cats   d) women
        e) pets

2 a) empty   b) crowded
   c) unique   d) normal
        e) quiet

3 a) enemy   b) library
   c) city   d) edge
        e) world

4 a) bridges   b) bays
   c) trees   d) buildings
        e) tunnels

5 a) ran   b) jogged
   c) joked   d) looked
        e) stumbled

6 a) grown   b) splashed
   c) erupted   d) disappeared
        e) switched

7 a) ships   b) planes
   c) cars   d) trains
        e) trucks

WILDFIRE

In an average year, several wildfires happen on the Sherburne National Wildlife Refuge. How often they happen and the size of these fires mostly depends on the weather.

Humans cause the most wildfires on the Refuge. Off the Refuge, many fires are started as a result of debris burning. Often, these fires ____1____. In some cases, this happens several days after a debris fire is thought to have gone out. Air temperature, wind speed, and humidity come together to make it easier for fires to burn again and spread.

Lightning causes fires to start on the Refuge. This happens about once every three or four years. Lightning generally comes with ____2____. Therefore, these fires do not usually grow to a large size. Often they are found by people as a smoldering stump where lightning has struck a tree in the woods and caused it to fall down. The stumps will smolder until they start to make enough smoke for someone to see and ____3____.

Human-caused fires that start on the Refuge are most often the result of someone starting the fire on purpose or of carelessness. These fires are usually stopped before they become large. However, some have spread over hundreds of acres. These ____4____ life and property off the Refuge.

The Sand Dunes State Forest Fire Tower keeps constant watch during periods of high fire danger. It is south of the Refuge. Fires are also often ____5____ in by sharp-eyed members of the public. These careful watchers might catch a glimpse smoke while out driving or hiking. Many people now carry cell phones. They have helped tremendously to increase the ____6____ at which the public can report a fire. This allows fire personnel to act while a fire is still small.

Due to the fairly small size of the Refuge and the surrounding urban area, all unplanned wildfires are put out as soon as ____7____. This lowers the risk to life and property.

1 a) finish   b) leave
    c) end   d) restart
      e) freeze

2 a) thunder   b) sleet
    c) snow   d) sun
      e) rain

3 a) whistle   b) ignite
    c) show   d) stomp
      e) report

4 a) threaten   b) sting
    c) ignore   d) undo
      e) hate

5 a) turned   b) called
    c) found   d) filled
      e) put

6 a) temperature   b) volume
    c) height   d) speed
      e) depth

7 a) taken   b) increased
    c) possible   d) lowered
      e) called

BAT BIOLOGY

Bats are not rodents. They ___1___ to their own special group of mammals called *Chiroptera*, which means "hand wing." Bat wings are actually a kind of finger bones attached by a thin skin membrane, or tissue.

Bats are more closely ___2___ to primates (monkeys, apes, and humans) than to rodents. Like other mammals, bats are warm-blooded and furry. They nurse their young.

Bats are the only mammals that truly fly. Bats are not blind. Like dolphins, they navigate, ___3___ obstacles, and find food using a very sophisticated system called echolocation. Echolocation works when a bat sends out high-frequency sounds that bounce off objects. The bat then hears the rebounding echo and reacts accordingly. This system is so good that bats can sense obstacles as small as a gnat or a human hair in total darkness. With such advanced methods, they are ___4___ to fly into people.

Connecticut bats mate in the fall and early winter. However, it isn't until spring when fertilization occurs. Pregnant bats then move from their winter hibernating sites (called hibernacula) to maternity sites or nursery colonies.

Most bats create a single baby bat every six to eight weeks after they mate. This is a very low reproductive rate for a small mammal. Thus, their populations are quite ___5___. When harmed, populations require a long time to recover.

Many bats do not breed until they are two years old. They may live for 30 years. Young bats grow ___6___. They are already able to fly within five weeks. While females are attending to the young in nursery colonies, males meet in separate groups called bachelor colonies.

Cold winter temperatures force many Connecticut bats to move during the winter. They usually travel less than 300 miles. Bats look for a ___7___ or other dark, secluded hibernating sites. The perfect temperature for hibernating bats varies from 41 to 58°F. Big brown bats, commonly found in buildings, can survive subzero temperatures. They may hibernate in walls, attics, cliff faces, and rock shelters.

1
a) hang
b) run
c) travel
d) belong
e) wave

2
a) related
b) hooked
c) concentrated
d) near
e) attached

3
a) avoid
b) destroy
c) hit
d) hurt
e) smash

4
a) trying
b) able
c) likely
d) used
e) unlikely

5
a) high
b) eager
c) large
d) strong
e) weak

6
a) slowly
b) rapidly
c) sideways
d) randomly
e) outwardly

7
a) cloud
b) cave
c) field
d) pool
e) bench

CONNECTICUT GETS A CHARTER

The people of Connecticut had decided to send their governor, Mr. John Winthrop, to England to get a charter for their colony. The new king, Charles II, was in power.

When Mr. Davenport heard of this, he ____1____ a letter to Governor Winthrop. He warned him not to include New Haven in the new charter. Mr. Winthrop replied that if the new charter did include New Haven, that colony could join Connecticut or not, as it pleased. He knew there were some people in the New Haven Colony who would be ____2____ to join Connecticut. These people were not happy with their own government.

Even New Haven Colony's own governor, Mr. William Leete, wrote to Mr. Winthrop. He said that he hoped the charter would include his colony. Mr. Leete was afraid that the king would ____3____ them in some way because they had hidden the men who helped bring about the death of the king's father. If they were joined to Connecticut, they would probably escape such a penalty.

Some of the English lords who had formerly owned the land helped Mr. Winthrop. They presented a valuable ring to the king. The ring had once belonged to the king's father, Charles I.

Governor Winthrop ____4____ in getting a charter for the colony of Connecticut. It was one of the best, if not the best, of the charters ____5____ to the New England colonies. It gave the people of Connecticut the right to govern themselves. They could elect their own officers and make all their own ____6____ without listening to the king.

That explains why, in 1688, when the governor of New England, Sir Edmund Andros, tried to take it away, the men of Hartford ____7____ it in the oak tree. The tree became known as the Charter Oak.

This colonial charter was so good that it was used by Connecticut as a state constitution for nearly 30 years after the formation of the Union.

1
a) recorded
b) illustrated
c) voiced
d) wrote
e) mapped

2
a) glad
b) miserable
c) mad
d) late
e) upset

3
a) help
b) lead
c) miss
d) forgive
e) punish

4
a) succeeded
b) failed
c) wallowed
d) missed
e) protested

5
a) moved
b) taken
c) driven
d) granted
e) checked

6
a) meals
b) streets
c) laws
d) buildings
e) statues

7
a) burned
b) hid
c) melted
d) smashed
e) shook

PRUDENCE CRANDALL AND THE CANTERBURY SCHOOL

In 1831, the people of Canterbury, Connecticut, made an offer to a 27-year-old woman. Her name was Prudence Crandall. The people of Canterbury wanted her to open a private school especially for young ____1____.

1 a) animals   b) citizens
    c) men   d) women
      e) nuns

Crandall accepted the ____2____. She had a ____3____ reputation as a teacher. She had gone to school at a Friends' Boarding School in Providence, Rhode Island. She had also been a teacher at some local schools. The Crandall family were Quakers from Rhode Island. They had moved to Canterbury when Prudence was young.

2 a) punishment   b) invitation
    c) present   d) explanation
      e) excuse

3 a) good   b) thin
    c) bad   d) quiet
      e) unknown

Prudence purchased an empty mansion. It was located on the town's green. She paid $500 as a down payment. The balance was a mortgage, or loan. It was for $1500.

The Canterbury Female Boarding School won the complete support of the community. It was soon a success. ____4____ taught included reading, writing, arithmetic, and English grammar. The female students also studied geography, history, chemistry, and astronomy. Basic tuition and room and board cost $100 per year. Students paid extra ____5____ for instruction in drawing, painting, music, and French. Crandall was able to pay off the $1500 mortgage within a year.

4 a) Words   b) Countries
    c) Songs   d) Books
      e) Subjects

5 a) fees   b) days
    c) chickens   d) vacations
      e) homework

At the time, white and African-American children received a free elementary education at the district schools. No further public or private education was made available to African-American children. Marcia Davis was Crandall's housekeeper. She told Crandall about how the African-American students were being separated from the whites.

Marcia and her friend Sarah Harris were both African Americans. Sarah's father was the local distributor of the *The Liberator*, an abolitionist newspaper. Marcia sometimes would leave ____6____ of the newspaper where Crandall would find them.

6 a) numbers   b) files
    c) copies   d) reporters
      e) typewriters

In the fall of 1832, Sarah Harris asked Crandall to let her into the Canterbury Female Boarding School. Harris hoped the education Crandall's academy ____7____ could help her and other African Americans. She wanted to return to Norwich, Connecticut as a teacher.

7 a) took   b) lost
    c) showed   d) found
      e) offered

    44

RED-HEADED WOODPECKER

Identification: The red-headed woodpecker is the only woodpecker in North America with an ____1____ red head and neck. Its back is solid black. Its belly is white. White inner wing patches and a white rump are especially noticeable while it is in flight. Young birds have a buff-brown or "dusky" head and back. Both males and females are similar in appearance. Its ____2____ is a high-pitched "queerk" and a rolling, repeated "kwurr-kwurr-kwurr."

1
a) outside   b) ugly
c) awful   d) entirely
        e) open

2
a) feeling   b) instrument
c) smell   d) flight
        e) call

Reason for Decline: A decline in farming and the loss of open woodlots have limited the amount of habitats for the red-headed woodpecker in Connecticut. The woodpecker has to ____3____ for good nesting places with the European starling bird. This has also added to the decline. The aggressive starlings often take over places found and prepared by woodpeckers.

3
a) hunt   b) shoot
c) compete   d) move
        e) bite

History in Connecticut: Since the mid-1800s, red-headed woodpeckers have nested in different locations across the state. Over time, old field and grassland habitats, large, old trees, and snags have disappeared. Therefore, red-headed woodpecker populations have declined. The red-headed woodpecker is now one of the rarest breeding birds in the area. The woodpeckers can be ____4____ in Connecticut in greater numbers during the fall. They don't often stay the winter here, unless acorns or other crops are ____5____.

4
a) felt   b) welcomed
c) heard   d) forgotten
        e) seen

5
a) purchased   b) available
c) missing   d) removed
        e) examined

Interesting Facts: Red-headed woodpeckers are less likely to drill for food than other woodpeckers. Instead, they fly down to the ground to catch insects. Or they catch ____6____ from the air. They have been known to wedge live beetles or grasshoppers into cracks in wood to store them for future use. They will also use holes in trees to store acorns for the winter. Like blue jays and crows, red-headed woodpeckers have been known to steal eggs from the nests of smaller birds.

6
a) diseases   b) water
c) sickness   d) shoes
        e) prey

Red-headed woodpeckers are often killed by ____7____ while searching for food along roads and highways.

7
a) vehicles   b) mammals
c) animals   d) birds
        e) hunters

Although most red-headed woodpeckers live in different places during different times of the year, some may remain year-round in warmer southern climates.

45

COUGARS IN THE APPALACHIANS?

Cougars (*Puma concolor*) are also known as mountain lions, pumas, panthers, painters, and catamounts. They were living throughout the eastern U.S. when European settlers arrived. Many Appalachian ___1___ tell of panthers following people, dropping on people from tree limbs, and covering a sleeping person with leaves.

1 a) mysteries   b) babies
   c) lies   d) dreams
       e) stories

By 1950, lots of ___2___ and logging had apparently wiped out the cougar population. However, people in isolated parts of the Appalachians still reported seeing them. Reports increased over time. By the 1990s, hard evidence began to build.

2 a) singing   b) hiking
   c) swimming   d) walking
       e) hunting

A home video taped in 1992 in western Maryland showed a cougar walking through the woods. In 1994, the U.S. Fish and Wildlife Service found a dropping in Vermont. It had cougar hair in it, which was probably swallowed while it was grooming itself. People in the Virginia Game Department reported cougar sightings in southwest Virginia in 1995. A plaster cast of a track in West Virginia in 1998 was confirmed to be from a cougar by a wildlife ___3___ in California.

3 a) expert   b) river
   c) animal   d) book
       e) sign

Some biologists and mountain people believe that a few native eastern cougars may have survived. In addition, there is proof that cougars caught in other places to be kept as pets have escaped or been ___4___. State and federal wildlife authorities now agree that at least some cougars are living wild in the Appalachians.

4 a) fired   b) eaten
   c) released   d) loved
       e) dead

Cougars are ___5___ and avoid humans. Many people live entire lifetimes in cougar country out west and never see one. Cougars are known to follow people sometimes, apparently out of curiosity. Fatal cougar attacks are extremely ___6___. Only a total of 13 people have been killed since 1890.

5 a) brave   b) shy
   c) violent   d) brutal
       e) extreme

6 a) common   b) rare
   c) believable   d) scary
       e) truthful

There are some simple ways to avoid problems if you find a cougar in the woods. Don't move too quickly because ___7___ triggers the cougars to chase. Open your arms to make yourself big. Speak loudly but calmly. Keep eye contact. Back away slowly, taking care not to trip. Cougars can be driven away by resistance. Best of all, stay close to an adult!

7 a) running   b) yelling
   c) laughing   d) walking
       e) whispering

NOTES

NOTES

Made in the USA
Lexington, KY
08 May 2019